THE FIRST BOOK OF SOPRANO SOLOS PART II

compiled by Joan Frey Boytim

ISBN 978-0-7935-2494-5

G. SCHIRMER, Inc.

DISTRIBUTED BY

HAL•LEONARD®
CORPORATION
7777 W. BLUEMOUND RD. P.O. BOX 13819 MILWAUKEE, WI 53213

PREFACE

The widespread acceptance by teachers and students of "The First Book Series" for Soprano, Mezzo-Soprano/Alto, Tenor, Baritone/Bass has prompted the development of a Part II addition for each voice type. After discussions with numerous voice teachers, the key suggestion expressed many times was that there is a need for "more of the same" type of literature at exactly the same level.

The volumes in Part II follow many of the same concepts which are covered in the Preface of the original volumes, including a comprehensive selection of between 34 and 37 songs from the Baroque through the 20th Century. The selections range from easy to moderate difficulty for both singer and accompanist.

In response to many requests, we have included more sacred songs, and have added two Christmas solos in each volume. The recommendation for more humorous songs for each voice was honored as well.

Even though these books have a heavy concentration of English and American songs, we have also expanded the number of Italian, German, and French offerings. For those using the English singing translations, we have tried to find the translations that are most singable, and in several cases have reworked the texts.

Part II can easily stand alone as a first book for a beginning high school, college, or adult student. Because of the varied contents, Part II can also be successfully used in combination with the first volume of the series for an individual singer. This will give many choices of vocal literature, allowing for individual differences in student personality, maturity, and musical development.

Hal Leonard Publishing (distributor of G. Schirmer) and Richard Walters, supervising editor, have been most generous in allowing the initial objective for this series to be expanded more fully through publishing these companion volumes. We hope this new set of books will provide yet another interesting and exciting new source of repertoire for both the teacher and student.

Joan Frey Boytim
September, 1993

About the Compiler...

Since 1968, Joan Frey Boytim has owned and operated a full-time voice studio in Carlisle, Pennsylvania, where she has specialized in developing a serious and comprehensive curriculum and approach to teaching and coaching adolescent and community adult students. Her teaching experience has also included music and choral instruction at the junior high and senior high levels, and voice instruction at the college level. She is the author of a widely used bibliography, *Solo Vocal Repertoire for Young Singers* (a publication of NATS), and, as a nationally recognized expert on teaching beginning vocal study, has been featured in many speaking engagements and presentations on the subject.

CONTENTS

ANIMAL CRACKERS

Christopher Morley

Richard Hageman

* From "Songs for a Little House", Copyright, 1917, by George H. Doran Company.

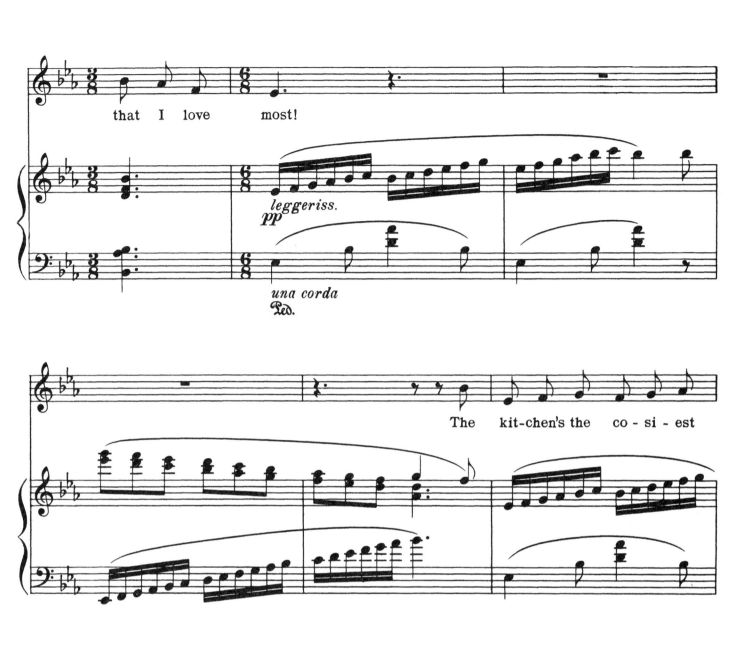

that I love most!

leggeriss.
pp

una corda
Ped.

The kit-chen's the co-si-est

place that I know: The ket-tle is sing-ing, the stove is a-glow, And

there in the twi - light, how jol - ly to see The co - coa and an - i - mals

wait - ing for me. Dad - dy and Moth - er dine lat - er in state, With

p

tre corde

Ma - ry to cook for them, Su - san to wait; But they don't have near - ly as

mf

much fun as I, Who eat in the kit-chen with Nurse stand-ing by; And

Lento   Tempo Iº

Dad-dy once said, he would like to be me, Hav-ing co-coa and an-i-mals

once more for tea!

COME AND TRIP IT

(from *L'Allegro*)

George Frideric Handel,
arranged by Mary Carmichael

Come and trip it as you go, On the light fan -

tas - tick. toe, trip it, trip it, Come and trip it

as you go, as

you go On the light fan - tas - tick toe.

Come and trip it as you go.

Come and trip it as you go

On the light fan _ tas _ tick toe, trip it, trip it,

Come and trip it as you go,

15

ANDENKEN
(I Think of Thee)

Friedrich von Matthison

Ludwig van Beethoven

Published in 1810.

I think of thee when thro' the grove the night-ingale's lovely
Ich den - ke dein, wenn durch den hain der Nach - ti - gal - len Ak -

notes are ring-ing; I think of thee! When,
kor - de schal-len! Wann denkst du mein? wann,

18

AVE MARIA
(O Lord, Most Holy)

Franz Abt

CHARMANT PAPILLON

(Charming Butterfly)

English text by
Mrs. O. B. Boise

André Campra

Charmant pa - pil - lon, dont l'ai - le d'or pas - se Dans____ l'es - pa -
Brilliant but - ter - fly, whose wings gai - ly glis - ten, Fair - - est flow -

- - - ce Comme u - ne fleur!
- - - ers dost thou out - vie!

Charmant pa - pil - lon, dont l'ai - le d'or pas - se Dans____ l'es -
Bril - liant but - ter - fly, whose wings gai - ly glis - ten, Fair - - est

pa - - - - - ce Comme u - ne fleur! Que ne
flow - - - - - ers dost thou out - vie! Would that

puis-je, sur ta tra - ce, M'en - vo - ler a - vec toi_____ com -
I might be thy com - rade! Ah, how glad-ly I'd fol - - low

me u - ne sœur!
thee for aye!

Char - mant pa - pil - lon, dont l'ai - le d'or pas - se Dans_____ l'es_
Bril - liant but - ter - fly, whose wings_gai - ly glis - ten, Fair - -est_

pa - - - - - - - ce Com - me u - ne
flow - - - - - - - ers dost thou out -

fleur;__ Je vou-drais_____ vo - ler a-vec
vie!__ I would glad - - - -ly,__ so glad-ly__

toi_____ com - me u - ne sœur!
fol - - - - - - -low thee for aye!

C'est à pei - ne si tu te__ po - ses,
With - out rest thou art ev - er__ flit - ting,

C'est à pei - ne si tu te po - ses
with - out rest thou art ev - er flit - ting,

Sur la feuil - le ten - dre des ro - ses, Dans l'es - pa -
From the bud - ding blush - ros - es sip - ping, Dost thou seek

- ce que tu par - cours. Ah!
- in their hearts re - pose? Ah!

- que tes bon jours Sont courts! Char - mant pa - pil - lon, dont l'ai - le d'or
- too soon thy life must close! Bril - liant but - ter - fly, whose wings gai - ly

COME TO THE FAIR

Helen Taylor

Easthope Martin

Lyrics: The sun is a-shin-ing to wel-come the day,

Heigh — ho! come to the fair! The folk are all sing-ing so mer-ry and gay,

*The Introduction may be commenced at the sign ◆

Heigh - ho! come to the fair! All the stalls on the green are as fine as can be__ With trink-ets and tok-ens so pret-ty to see, So it's come then, maid-ens and men, To the fair in the pride of the morn - ing__ So deck your-selves out in your fin-est ar - ray, With a heigh - ho!__

For love mak-ing too, if so be you've a mind, Heigh -
ho! come to the fair! For hearts that are hap-py are lov-ing and kind,
Heigh - ho! come to the fair! If "Haste to the wed-ding" the fid-dles should play, I
war-rant you'll dance to the end of the day;— Come then, maid-ens and men To the

fair in the pride of the morn - ing The sun is a-shin-ing to wel-come the

day, With a heigh - ho! come to the fair, Maid-ens and men,

maid-ens and men, Come to the fair in the morn - ing, Heigh -

ho_____ come to the fair!_____

THE CRYING OF WATER

Arthur Symons

Louis Campbell-Tipton

All night   long_____   cry - ing
Et   la   nuit_____   s'é - meut

with mourn - ful   cry.
de   ta   dou - leur.

Dis-

As   I   lie   and   lis - ten,_____   and
moi   si   ta   cla - meur_____   Et

40

42

HERE AMID THE SHADY WOODS

Thomas Morell

George Frideric Handel
(1685 - 1759)

44

DRIFT DOWN, DRIFT DOWN

(Winter)

Harold Simpson

Landon Ronald

Drift down, drift down from the skies, Lit-tle white snow-flakes fall-ing fast,

Like sleep that falls on tired eyes To bring us peace at last: Drift down, drift down

from the skies, Lit-tle white snow - flakes, Lit-tle white snow-flakes fall-ing

fast.

GESÙ BAMBINO
(The Infant Jesus)

Frederick H. Martens

Pietro Yon

When

blos - soms flow - ered 'mid __ the snows U - pon a win - ter night __ Was

born __ the Child, __ the Christ - mas Rose, The King __ of Love __ and Light. __ The

an - gels sang, __ the shep - herds sang, The grate - ful earth __ re - joiced, ____

And at __ His bless - ed birth the stars Their ex - ul - ta - tion

Non troppo lento

voiced. _____ O come let us a -
Opt: *Ve - ni - te a - do -*

54

GRANDMA

Leonard Feeney

Theodore Chanler

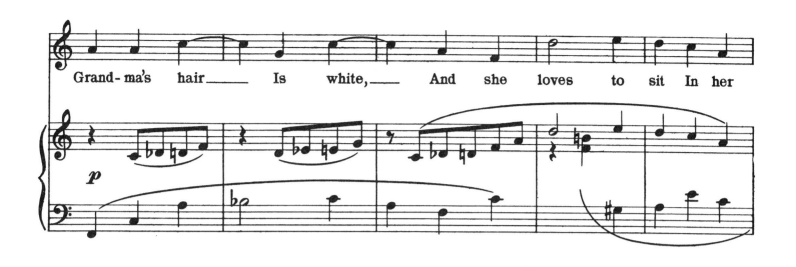

Grand-ma's hair__ Is white,__ And she loves to sit In her

rock-ing-chair,__ And knit And talk And al - most rock,

sempre pp

And see you dim - ly__ with her poor eye - sight.

Grand-ma says____ That

God Is good, But that His ways Are odd And can-not be

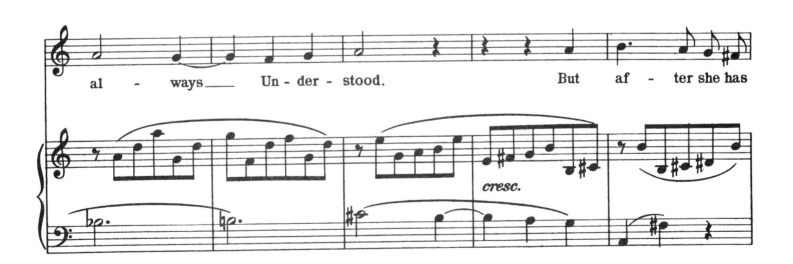

al - ways____ Un-der-stood. But af - ter she has

tak - en a cook-ie from the shelf, And giv-en it to you And

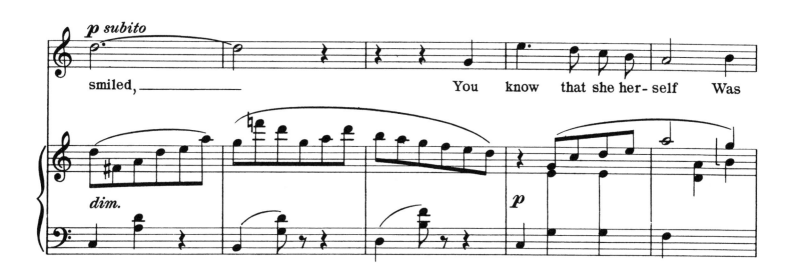

p subito

smiled,_____ You know that she her-self Was

un poco rubato

once a lit - tle child, And had a grand-ma too._____

L'HEURE EXQUISE
(The Hour of Dreaming)

translation by Theodore Baker

Reynaldo Hahn

Tranquillo e dolce possibile

La lu - ne blan - che Luit dans les bois;
The moon - beams whit - en Boughs all a - round,

De cha - que bran - che Part u - ne voix Sous la ra -
Wher-e'er they light - en Voic - es re - sound Dim in the

mé - e...
gloam - ing:

62

HOW LOVELY ARE THY DWELLINGS

Psalm 54

Samuel Liddle

O Lord God of Hosts, hear my prayer. I would ra - ther be a door - keep-er in the house of my God, than to dwell in the tents of wick - ed - ness .... For a day in Thy courts is bet - ter than a thou - sand. How

p

pp [Organ alone]

cresc

con fervore

mf [Piano and Organ]

f

Tempo primo.

love - ly are Thy dwell - ings, O Lord of

Ped. ✻ Ped. ✻

Hosts! My soul long - eth yea faint - eth, for the

courts of the Lord: my heart and my flesh cry

mf

out for the liv - - ing God

rit.

67

ICH LIEBE DICH
(I Love You)

Poem by Herrosee
English by
Lorraine Noel Finley

Ludwig van Beethoven

INTORNO ALL'IDOL MIO

(Caressing Mine Idol's Pillow)

English version by
Theodore Baker

Marco Antonio Cesti

Al mio ben, che ri - po - sa su l'a - li
To my love, who his spir - it to rest - ful

del - la quie - te, gra - ti, gra - ti
night doth sur - ren - der, Waft ye, waft ye

so - gni as - si - ste - te, E il mio racchiu - so ar -
fair dreams and ten - der, And all my pas - sion re -

do - re sve - la - te - gli per me, o lar - ve, o
press - ed Re - veal to him for me, O vis - ion, O

LACHEN UND WEINEN
(Laughing and Crying)

Friedrich Rückert
translation by Joan Boytim

Franz Schubert

Etwas geschwind

pp

La - chen und Wei - nen zu jeg - li - cher Stun - de
Laugh - ing and cry - ing my heart___ has its sea - sons;

ruht ___ bei der Lieb ___ auf so man - cher - lei Grun - de.
Where ___ is the cu - pid who knows ___ all the rea - sons?

wußt, ist mir selb'____ nicht be - wußt.
know, *I* *my - self* ____ *do* *not* *know.*

pp

Wei - nen und
Cry - ing and

La - chen,
laugh - ter?

muß ich dich fra - - gen, o
It's on - ly you, O heart, can

Herz, muß ich dich fra - gen, o Herz.
tell, it's on - ly you, O heart, can tell.

THE LAST ROSE OF SUMMER

Thomas Moore

Richard Alfred Miliken
Setting by Friedrich Von Flotow

Larghetto

'Tis the last rose ___ of ___ sum - mer, Left ___ bloom - ing a - lone. All her love - ly ___ com - pan - ions are ___ fa - ded and ___ gone. ___ No ___ flow - er of her kin - dred, No ___ rose - bud is nigh, _____ To re -

flect back ___ her ___ blush - es, Or ___ give ___ sigh for sigh!

I'll not leave thee, ___ thou ___ lone one, To ___

pine ___ on the stem, Since the love - ly ___ are ___ sleep - ing, Go ___

sleep ___ thou with them. Thus ___ kind - ly I scat - ter Thy ___

leaves _____ o'er the bed, _____ Where thy mates of _____ the _____

gar - den Lie _____ scent - less and dead, Where thy

cresc.

mates of _____ the _____ gar - den Lie _____ scent - less and

f　　　　　　　　　　　　　　　　　　　　　　*dim.*

dead.

NO FLOWER THAT BLOWS

Thomas Linley

Printed in the USA by G. Schirmer, Inc.

No flow'r that blows is like, is like this rose,＿

no flow'r that blows＿ is like, is like this rose, Dear

pledge＿ to prove a pa - rent's love, A pleas - ing,

pleas - ing gift＿ thou art; Come, sweet-est flow'r, and

from＿ this hour Live hence-forth in my heart, live hence-forth in my

heart. No flow'r that blows is like, is like this

rose,＿ no flow'r that blows＿ is like, is like this

rose.

A NUN TAKES THE VEIL

Gerard Manley Hopkins

Samuel Barber

And I have asked to be Where

no storms come, Where the green swell is in the ha-vens dumb,

And out of the swing of the sea.

NUR WER DIE SEHNSUCHT KENNT

(None But the Lonely Heart)

Johann Wolfgang von Goethe
Translated by Arthur Westbrook

Pytor Il'yichTchaikovsky

None but the lone - ly heart
Nur wer die Sehn - sucht kennt,

Can know my sad - ness;_____ A - lone, and
weiss, was ich lei - del_____ Al - lein und

ORPHEUS WITH HIS LUTE

from *Henry VIII* by William Shakespeare

William Schuman

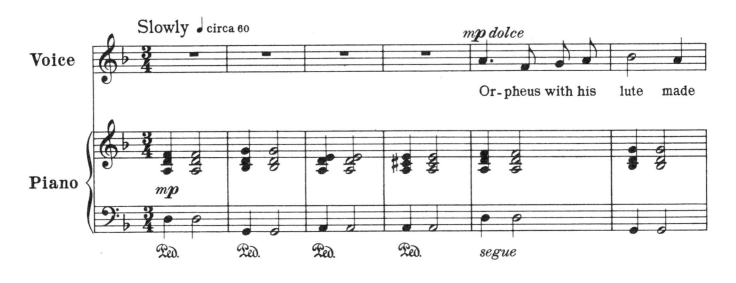

show'rs There had made a last-ing spring. _____ Ev-'ry thing that heard him

play, E-ven the bil-lows of the sea, Hung their heads, and then lay

by. _____ In sweet mu-sic is such art, Kill-ing care and grief of

heart, Fall a-sleep, or hear-ing, die. _____

New Rochelle, N.Y.
August 6, 1944

O SAVIOUR, HEAR ME!

Christoph Willibald Gluck,
arranged by Dudley Buck

Dudley Buck

turn ____ on me ____ thy lov - ing eyes;

Lord ____ I ___ long ___ for thy ____ sal - va - -tion,

And ____ would fain ___ at - tain ___ the ____

1.
prize.

2.
prize, ____ *rall.* *pp*

rall. - - - - - *pp*

LA PASTORELLA
The Shepherd Maid

Carlo Goldoni
English text by
Lorraine Noel Finley

Franz Schubert

pa - sto - rel - la al pra - to con - ten - ta se __ ne __
shep - herd maid sang bright - ly A __ song __ that filled the __

va, coll' a - gnel - li - no a la - to can -
lea, While lambs were frol - ick - ing light - ly, Her __

tan - do in li - ber - tà, _____ can - tan - do in li - ber -
heart __ was fan - cy - free, _____ Her heart __ was fan - cy -

tà, _____ can - tan - do in li - ber - tà.
free, _____ Her heart __ was fan - cy - free.

PETIT NOËL
(Little Noel)

Theophile Gautier
English version by
Margaret Aliona Dole

Emile Louis

him   smiles up-on his   face sub - lime._____

lui   son__ vi - sa - ge char - mant._____

Bells, gay-ly chime a fes-tal song!_____ The Christ is born! The

Clo - ches, ca - ril-lon-nez gaî - ment!_____ Jé - sus est né, Jé -

poco rit.

p a tempo

Christ is born!_____ No warm, white cov-'ring in the

sus est né._____ Pas de cour - ti - nes fes-tòn -

poco rit.

a tempo

man - ger   To keep the Babe from bit - ter   cold;_____

né - es   Pour pré - ser - ver l'enfant du froid;_____

THE PRAYER PERFECT

James Whitcomb Riley

Oley Speaks

*From Rhymes of Childhood, Copyright 1890, 1928. Used by special permission of the publishers, The Bobbs-Merrill Co.

Scat-ter ev-'ry care — Down a wake of an - gel wings Win-now-ing the air. Dear Lord, kind Lord! Gra-cious Lord! I pray— Thou wilt look on all I love Ten-der-ly to - day.

Bring un-to the sor - row-ing All re-lease from pain, Let the lips of laugh - ter O - ver-flow a - gain,

And with all the need - y O di-vide, I pray,— This vast trea-sure

of con-tent That is mine to - day! Dear Lord, kind Lord!

Gra-cious Lord! I pray___ Thou wilt look on all I love Ten - der - ly to -

day.

PER NON PENAR

(For My Heart's Peace)

Emanuele d'Astorga

English text by Nathan Haskell Dole

Per non pe - nar non la - sce-ró d'a-mar,
For my heart's peace My love will nev-er cease!

per non pe - nar non la_sce-ró d'a-mar; sem-pre co -
For my heart's peace My love will nev-er cease; Hum-bly de-

Printed in the USA by G. Schirmer, Inc.

110

TO A WILD ROSE

Hermann Hagedorn

Edward MacDowell
Transcribed by
R. H. Elkin

113

QUELLA BARBARA CATENA
(This Hard Bondage)

English version by Nathan Kaskell Dole

Francesco Ciampi

rò,— io di - rò che non dà pe - na, io di - rò,— io di - rò,— io di -
boast, I can boast it nev - er pains me, I can boast, I can boast, I can

rò— che non dà pe - na, ma un so - a - ve e bel— pia - cer,
boast it nev - er pains me,. Rath - er gives me keen de - light;

no, no, i - o di - rò— che non dà pe - na,
ay! ay! I— can boast it nev - er pains me,

co‿ re io di - rò‿ che non dà pe - na, io di - rò‿ che non dà
bos-om, I can boast it nev - er pains me, I can boast it nev - er

pe - na, io di - rò‿ che non‿ dà pe - na, ma un so - a - ve e bel‿ pia-
pains me, I can boast it nev - er pains me, Rath-er it gives me keen de-

cer, non fa stra - zio, non dà pe - na, quel-la bar - ba - ra‿ ca -
light. This hard bond-age that en - chains me, I can boast it nev - er

te - na,   io   di - ro__   che   non   dà   pe - na, ma un so - a - vee bel__ pia -
pains me,   I   can   boast it   nev - er   pains me, Rath-er it   gives me   keen de-

cer,   e bel__ pia - cer,   e bel__ pia -
light,   a   keen de - light,   a   keen de-

cer.
light!

ROMANCE

Paul Bourget
Translation by
M. Louise Baum

Claude Debussy

Moderato

L'âme é - va - po - rée et souf - fran - te, L'â - me dou - ce, l'âme o - do - ran - te Des lis di - vins __ que j'ai cueil - lis Dans le jar - din de ta pen - sée, Où donc les vents l'ont - ils chassée Cette âme a - do - ra - ble des lis?

Ev - a - nes-cent breath of the lil - y, Ten-der fan - cies, O fra - grant spir - it of heav'n-ly lays, __ Which I in-hal'd 'mid gar-den-ways Of thy dear soul; Where is it fled on wings of air, Thy soul lil - y-pure, and so fair?

121

SELIGKEIT
(Bliss)

Ludwig Heinrich Christoph Hölty

Franz Schubert

1. Freu-den son-der Zahl_____ blüh'n im Him-mels-saal_____
2. Je-dem lä-chelt traut_____ ei-ne Him-mels-braut;_____
3. Lie-ber bleib' ich hier,_____ lä-chelt Lau-ra mir_____

1. *Joy and peace and love_____ reign in Heav'n a-bove:_____*
2. *Each one at his side_____ has a heav'n-ly bride;_____*
3. *I would ra-ther stay_____ here, with thee! says May,_____*

123

SOLVEJG'S SONG

Henrik Ibsen
English version by Arthur Westbrook

Edvard Grieg

Printed in the USA by G. Schirmer, Inc.

125

A SPIRIT FLOWER

B. Martin Stanton

Louis Campbell-Tipton

They seemed to whis-per soft-ly thy dear name; _____ They
Zer-flie - ssend flüs-tern sie mir zu von dir, _____ Wie

melt-ed with the tear-drops from mine eyes. But
Thrä-nen rin-nend von der Wan - ge mir. Doch

sud-den-ly there bloomed, with - in that hour, In my poor heart, so
plötzlich fühl-te ich mein Herz er - glüh'n, Und sah im Schnee ein

* Singers desiring to sing the _f×_ should strike out the _b_ in the piano part

WHEN DAISIES PIED

"Love's Labour's Lost"
William Shakespeare

Thomas Augustine Arne

1. When dai-sies pied, and
2. When shep-herds pipe on

vi-o-lets blue, And la-dy smocks all sil-ver white, And cuck-oo buds of
oat-en straws, And mer-ry larks are plough-men's clocks, And tur-tles tread, and

yel-low hue, Do paint the mead-ows with ___ de-light:
rooks, ___ and daws, And maid-ens bleach ___ their sum-mer frocks:

Printed in the USA by G. Schirmer, Inc.

WHEN I WAS SEVENTEEN

H. Lilljebjörn
English version by Marion Bromley Newton

Swedish Folksong

*) These variants are by Madame Sembrich.